I0866709

COLORADO Wildflowers

MONTANE ZONE

THE COLORADO MOUNTAIN CLUB GUIDEBOOK

COLORADO Wildflowers

MONTANE ZONE

Ann Kurz Chambers

The Colorado Mountain Club Press
Golden, Colorado

Colorado Wildflowers—Montane Zone

PUBLISHED BY
The Colorado Mountain Club Press
710 Tenth Street, #200, Golden, Colorado 80401
303-996-2743; 800-633-4417 | email: cmcpress@cmc.org | www.cmc.org

Founded in 1912, The Colorado Mountain Club is the largest outdoor recreation, education, and conservation organization in the Rocky Mountains. Look for our books at your local bookstore or outdoor retailer or online at www.cmc.org.

CONTACTING THE PUBLISHER
We would appreciate it if readers would alert us to any errors or outdated information by contacting us at the address above.

Alan Bernhard	design, composition, and production
Michelle Myers	copyeditor
Susan Hill Newton	proofreader
Alan Stark	publisher

Cover painting: Mule's Ears, *Asteraceae Wyethia amplexicaulis*, by Ann Kurz Chambers

DISTRIBUTED TO THE BOOK TRADE BY
Mountaineers Books
1001 SW Klickitat Way, Suite 201, Seattle, WA 98134
800-553-4453 | www.mountaineersbooks.org

We gratefully acknowledge the financial support of the people of Colorado through the Scientific and Cultural Facilities District of greater metropolitan Denver for our publishing activities.

First Edition

ISBN 978-0-9842213-0-1

Printed in Korea

Dedication

To my children,

to their children,

and to their children's children,

in perpetuity.

CONTENTS

WHITE FLOWERS

YELLOW FLOWERS

RED, ORANGE, AND PINK FLOWERS

BLUE FLOWERS

PURPLE FLOWERS

GREEN AND BROWN FLOWERS

Acknowledgment

A special thank you to my daughter Phoebe,
for her help in manuscript preparation.

ALSO BY ANN KURZ CHAMBERS

Cranberries from A to Z,
An Educational Picture Book,
by Ann Kurz

Coming Home to Door
by Amanda Brekke (pseudonym);
contributing author, Ann Kurz Chambers

Another special thank you to Alan Stark
for his vision and confidence
in how special this book could be.
By publishing this book
he has validated all my years of work
for which I will be forever grateful.

"Do what you can, with what you have, where you are."

THEODORE ROOSEVELT

PROLOGUE

This book is a pictorial documentation of flowering wild plants growing at "the cabin" located on my thirty-five-acre mountain property in Eagle County, Colorado. The impetus for this project was my wish to assemble a point-in-time record of flowering plants that have endured on my property after centuries of livestock grazing and human activity. I discovered and recorded the specimens through 2008.

I had expected to discover that all the flowering plants I found were native, or indigenous, to the area. I was surprised to learn that several plants on my property are classified as non-natives or aliens from Europe or Asia. Some were accidental immigrants, carried to North America unintentionally, while others were purposely introduced. I was disappointed that I did not find a columbine, the Colorado state flower. I hope that a dormant or wind-blown seed will find conditions favorable for a return to its native area. Several of the non-native plants are my nemeses: I work every year to keep my property free of cheat grass, thistles, and other invasive and undesirable aliens.

My lifelong interest in pursuing wildflowers was fostered by easy access to the forest surrounding my Wisconsin childhood home. Trillium, violet, and jack-in-the-pulpit thrived in large patches there. As a child, I was inspired to save some wildflowers before they were destroyed by home developers clearing the forest. I transplanted them to our backyard in a small undeveloped area my mother chose to leave as "wild" when our house was built in 1948. I clearly remember when I was nine and ten years old setting myself to this self-imposed task, filled with energy and enthusiasm. I dragged my wagon over rough paths through the woods, dug up plants, lifted the heavy clumps into the wagon, and bore them home triumphantly.

This childhood determination to value and save wildflowers formed a lasting impression, and was subsequently manifested in this documentation project. In the interim between childhood and today, I became an artist. I specialized in painting wildflowers and plants of Wisconsin, including a focus on cranberry plants and culture. I was again a plant hunter, this time not saving them from destruction, but painting them, thereby elevating wild plants to the importance I felt they deserved. This life-long and passionate wildflower interest has been a motivating force, a common thread, in my life. Moreover, I have a special and personal interest in finding them on my cabin property. These feelings have been further enhanced through many years of work and focus on this project.

INTRODUCTION

There are five distinct plant life zones in Colorado. The PLAINS (elevation 3,599 feet), the FOOTHILLS (elevation 6,000 feet), the MONTANE (elevation 8,000 feet), the SUB-ALPINE (elevation 10,000 feet), and the ALPINE (elevation 11,500 feet). My thirty-five acres span elevations between 8,260 feet and 8,650 feet, in the Montane zone. The aspen groves on my property are a good example of a typical Montane zone in Colorado, with a supporting understory of grasses, sedges, flowering plants, serviceberry, chokecherry, willow, snowberry, sagebrush, rabbit brush, Gambel oak, and Douglas fir.

To illustrate the various levels of moisture typically found in the Montane zone, and found on my property in particular, I have included two illustrated maps that follow this introduction. I included these supplements to be used as references for plant and trail locations and to provide a "lay-of-the-land" visualization of the thirty-five acres.

The Moisture Map indicates the moisture levels I have observed over several years. Many of the wildflowers are located in a moist, open woods area that I have named the "Hellebore Swamp." The name was inspired by the abundant presence of White False Hellebore plants. I think that this area is a microclimate; an area unique from the land surrounding it. In the Hellebore Swamp I have found a wide variety and number of specimens that favor the area's usually reliable levels of moisture. That area also supports aspen, serviceberry, and chokecherry, which together form an impenetrable jumble on the east and southeast sides, intermixed with thickets of oak and shrubs. A ridge to the north and to the west results in drainage of water into this area, which creates, essentially, a sump. From this sump, groundwater continues downhill, emerging in seeps and marshy areas of sedges and grasses. Eventually, water collects in two seasonally filled ponds.

In April and May, the Hellebore Swamp is saturated, and standing water has to be dodged to avoid wet feet. By midsummer, some places are still damp or wet, while the slightly higher hummocks have begun to dry. In late August, the swamp has little surface moisture. After years of observation, I have concluded that the Hellebore Swamp is an unusual area with many characteristics that favor the survival of indigenous plants. These naturally occurring features have allowed native plants to persevere through years of livestock grazing and other human activity. Two other areas sustain several varieties of wildflowers: the moist, shady woodland of Douglas fir and aspen, and the "top"—a dry, rocky mesa-like area at the apex and highest elevation of the property.

Over a period of 10 years, I found and subsequently identified 160 different flowering plants on my property. For ease of use, the wildflowers are organized by color (a subjective judgment) and then by family, genus, and species. During the early years of owning my land, I casually observed many wildflowers. However, with this documentation project, I devoted countless hours through spring and summer to discover the specimens. I canvassed my land, cutting several trails to access unexplored areas. Because the upper area of my acreage is wild, I took pepper spray as a precaution in case I had an encounter with a bear or mountain lion. A few years ago, a mountain lion followed me all day. On my hikes, I took water, snacks, a cell phone, a sketch book, and plastic bags to transport my finds back to the studio.

When I found a new flower, the next step was to identify it. I did this by consulting several reference books. Identifying and naming a plant could take minutes, or it could take hours, depending on the species. All plants are organized using well-established botanical rules. I used these rules to identify and label each specimen. Each specimen is identified first by family, then by genus within each family, and last by species within each genus.

A family encompasses plants with shared botanical characteristics. Within a family, groups of similar plants form a genus. All plants in the genus that look somewhat alike are called species. Every genus is named by a single capitalized Latin word. The various species of that genus are named by two words: the first is the capitalized name of the genus and the second word is a lowercase descriptive name, also in Latin.

Botanical rules specify that all species are to be named in Latin. Common English names can be wrong or confusing. The agreed upon Latin names provide definitive clarity. Moreover, common English names may describe different plants in different geographical areas. This book uses Latin species' names as well as common names on each painting. The common names used here are those found in several Colorado wildflower publications. For definitive identification however, one has to refer to the Latin names, especially when a genus includes several species. Moreover, Latin naming makes it possible to have a sensible way to have a dialogue about the huge, sometimes confusing, plant world.

I created the paintings from drawings of actual specimens in situ and/or in the studio. All specimens collected have been pressed and dried for future reference. I made a conscientious effort to paint and identify each plant correctly. But I concede to others more expert than I that misidentification may have occurred with a few confusing species. My field notes were written at the time of the observation and identification of each specimen. These brief notations contain relevant and pertinent aids to identification, or provide additional, interesting information.

I was amazed and delighted with the large number and variety of wild flowering plants I found. Some were readily visible, while others were so tiny they could easily have been missed. I continue to walk my property with a hopeful anticipation of discovering more specimens. I'm elated when I discover a new flower. I get further joy when I identify one more wildflower that lives on my small piece of western Colorado land.

Maybe one day, I'll find a columbine.

ANN KURZ CHAMBERS

SUMMER 2009

LEGEND

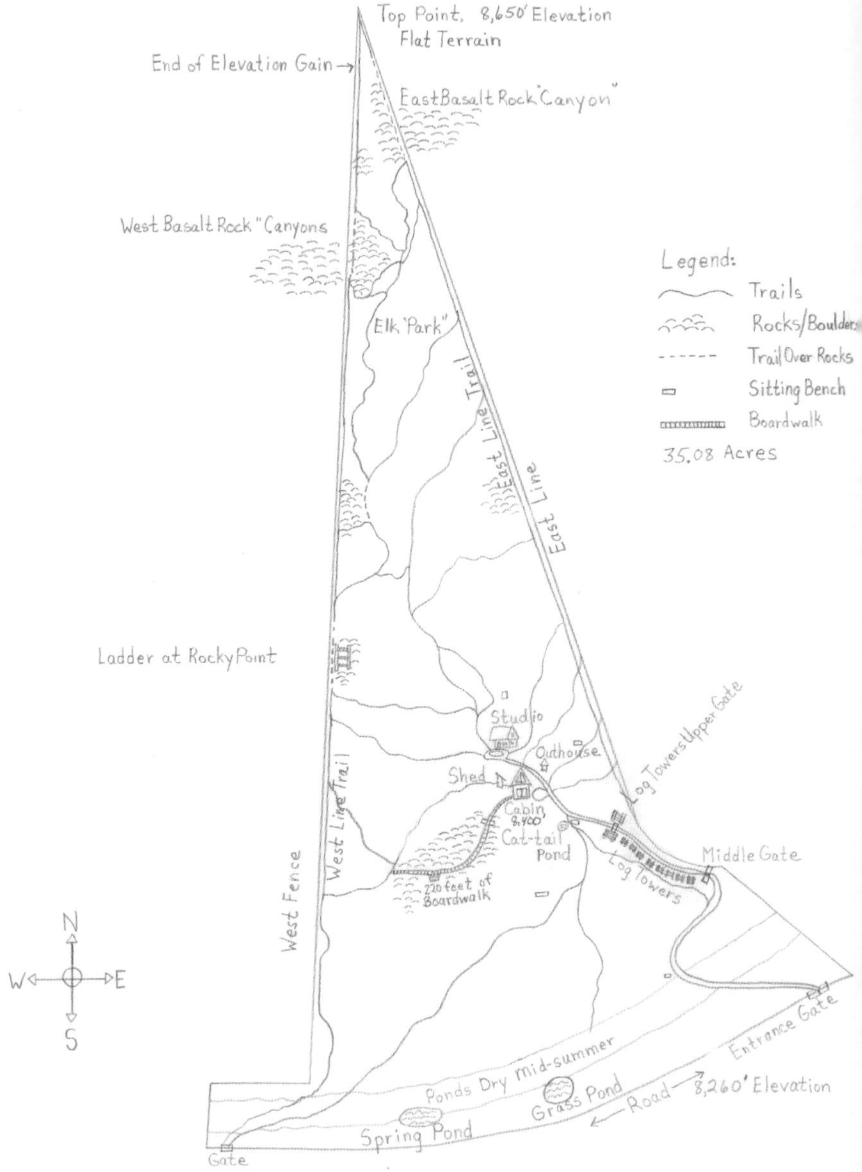

Top Point, 8,650' Elevation
Flat Terrain
End of Elevation Gain
East Basalt Rock "Canyon"
West Basalt Rock "Canyons
Elk "Park"
East Line Trail
East Line
Legend:
Trails
Rocks/Boulders
Trail Over Rocks
Sitting Bench
Boardwalk
35.08 Acres
Ladder at Rocky Point
Studio
Outhouse
Log Towers Upper Gate
Shed
Cabin
8,400'
Cat-tail
Pond
Log Towers
Middle Gate
West Line Trail
West Fence
220 feet of
Boardwalk
N
W
E
S
Ponds Dry mid-summer
Entrance Gate
Grass Pond
Road
8,260' Elevation
Spring Pond
Gate

MOISTURE MAP AND TYPICAL PLANT LOCATIONS

White Flowers

FAMILY: Parsley (*Apiaceae*)
GENUS: *Conioselinum*
SPECIES: *scopulorum*
COMMON NAME: Wild Celery

FIELD NOTES: Smooth, stiff, purplish ⅜-inch hollow stem with carrot-like leaves that smell like celery; top white umbel 3–6 inches in diameter. Wooded, moist areas. 4 feet. July–August. USDA: Rocky Mountain Hemlock Parsley

FAMILY: Parsley (*Apiaceae*)
GENUS: *Cryptotaenia*
SPECIES: *canadensis*
COMMON NAMES: Wild Chervil, Honewort

FIELD NOTES: 5 tiny, almost insignificant petals. Widely dispersed in shady woods. 1–4 feet. Blossoms in June–August; 1-inch seed pod follows blossoming.

FAMILY: Parsley (*Apiaceae*)
GENUS: *Orogenia*
SPECIES: *linearifolia*
COMMON NAME: Salt-and-Pepper

FIELD NOTES: White, tiny, dense umbel with "pepper" dots that are stamens; very delicate and innocuous. I found it with snow still in patches around it. Moist areas. 6 inches. April. USDA: Great Basin Indian Potato

FAMILY: Aster (*Asteraceae*)
GENUS: *Achillea*
SPECIES: *millefolium*
COMMON NAME: Yarrow

FIELD NOTES: Aromatic when leaves are crushed. Grows in clumps. Can be used as antiseptic and bug repellent. Dry areas. 8–30 inches. June–September. 20 percent of central mountains and plains flowers are in the *Asteraceae* family according to Rickett, 1973, who wrote, "From North Dakota to Oklahoma and west to the Cascade Mountains and the Sierra Nevada there are nearly 850 species," of *Asteraceae*. USDA: Western Yarrow

FAMILY: Aster (*Asteraceae*)
GENUS: *Antennaria*
SPECIES: *neglecta*
COMMON NAME: Pussytoes

FIELD NOTES: Dry, rocky, open areas. 6-8 inches. Late June.

FAMILY: Aster (*Asteraceae*)
GENUS: *Cirsium*
SPECIES: *neomexicanum*
COMMON NAME: Utah Thistle

FIELD NOTES: Disturbed ground. 3 feet. Mid-July.
USDA: Spiny Plumeless Thistle

FAMILY: Aster (*Asteraceae*)
GENUS: *Eucephalus*
SPECIES: *engelmannii*
COMMON NAME: Engelmann Aster

FIELD NOTES: Stiff stem, reddish on lower part of stem, leaves longer at base with pairs of leaves in larger leaf axils. Moist, open woods. 18 inches. Late August. USDA: Engelmann's Daisy

FAMILY: Aster (*Asteraceae*)
GENUS: *Erigeron*
SPECIES: *coulteri*
COMMON NAME: Coulter's Daisy

FIELD NOTES: Pure white with a yellow center and 30 petals. Moist, open areas. 18 inches. Late July.
USDA: Large Mountain Fleabane

FAMILY: Aster (*Asteraceae*)
GENUS: *Symphyotrichum*
SPECIES: *junceus*
COMMON NAME: Rush Aster

FIELD NOTES: Bloom 1¼ inch diameter, blossoms of white rays with ¼-inch disk with gold stamens. 24–25 petals. The leaves, stems, and flowers of many aster species are eaten by deer and elk. Damp areas. 1–3 feet. July.

FAMILY: Aster (*Asteraceae*)
GENUS: *Erigeron*
SPECIES: *vetensis*
COMMON NAME: Daisy

FIELD NOTES: Flower bud pinky lavender, ⅞-inch diameter white blossom. Hot, dry areas. 6–10 inches. June–July.
USDA: Early Bluetop Fleabane

FAMILY: Mustard (*Brassicaceae*)
GENUS: *Arabis*
SPECIES: *glabra*
COMMON NAMES: Arabis, Tower Rockcress

FIELD NOTES: 4 tiny white blossoms at top of stalk that mature into pine needle-like seed pods. Open meadows, sunny, dry, grassy areas. 30 inches. May-June.

FAMILY: Mustard (*Brassicaceae*)
GENUS: *Arabis*
SPECIES: *holboellii*
COMMON NAMES: Rockcress, Holboell's Cress

FIELD NOTES: 4 tiny white 1/32-inch petals. Seed pods hang down on opposite sides of stem. Dry, rocky, open areas. 2-3 feet. Late June. USDA: Holboell's Rockcress

FAMILY: Mustard (*Brassicaceae*)
GENUS: *Capsella*
SPECIES: *bursa-pastoris*
COMMON NAME: Shepherd's Purse

FIELD NOTES: Non-native. *Capsella* means "little box." Dry, disturbed ground. 6-16 inches. June.

FAMILY: Mustard (*Brassicaceae*)
GENUS: *Cardaria*
SPECIES: *draba*
COMMON NAMES: Hoary Cress, Whitetop Cress

FIELD NOTES: Aggressive alien. Dry, disturbed ground.
8-20 inches. June. USDA: Whitetop

FAMILY: Mustard (*Brassicaceae*)
GENUS: *Draba*
SPECIES: *lanceolata*
COMMON NAME: Lanceleaf Draba

FIELD NOTES: 4 petals, ⅜-inch flowers at top of stem. Leaves and stem are bristly, some with forked hairs. Open, grassy, wet meadows. 12 inches. Early June.

FAMILY: Mustard (*Brassicaceae*)
GENUS: *Thlaspi*
SPECIES: *arvense*
COMMON NAME: Field Pennycress

FIELD NOTES: Very recognizable in seed stage with ½-inch heart-shaped pod, notched at top. Weedy. Thrives in waste places, disturbed ground. 12–18 inches. June–September.

FAMILY: Pink (*Caryophyllaceae*)
GENUS: *Arenaria*
SPECIES: *congesta*
COMMON NAME: Congesta

FIELD NOTES: Grows in clumps. Umbel ½-inch across of congested, closely clustered flowers. 4-10 inches. May-August. USDA: Ballhead Sandwort

FAMILY: Pink (*Caryophyllaceae*)
GENUS: *Pseudostellaria*
SPECIES: *jamesiana*
COMMON NAME: James Starwort

FIELD NOTES: Common but often overlooked with trailing stems, delicate. Grows in clumps. Open, grassy, sunny areas. 16 inches. Late June.

FAMILY: Heath (*Ericaceae*)
GENUS: *Arctostaphylos*
SPECIES: *uva-ursi*
COMMON NAMES: Kinnickinnick, Bearberry

FIELD NOTES: A shrub with urn-shaped blossoms drooped at terminus of stem. This woody evergreen forms extensive mats of plants over dry, rocky areas. Shiny, leathery leaves. Fruit edible but unpalatable. To 12 inches. Blossoms in mid-May; red, ripe fruit in late July.

FAMILY: Bean (*Fabaceae*)
GENUS: *Lathyrus*
SPECIES: *lanszwertii*
COMMON NAME: Vetch

FIELD NOTES: Pea-like vines with rich, green leaves; 3 blossoms on each stem. Seeps, moist areas. 15 inches. June. USDA: Nevada Pea

FAMILY: Bean (*Fabaceae*)
GENUS: *Lupinus*
SPECIES: *arbustus*
COMMON NAME: Lupine

FIELD NOTES: Racemes 3-8 inches long, 7-11 leaf segments. Open woods. 12-15 inches. June.

FAMILY: Bean (*Fabaceae*)
GENUS: *Trifolium*
SPECIES: *longipes*
COMMON NAME: Clover

FIELD NOTES: Flower head on slender stalk, fragrant. Moist, open woods. 12 inches. Early June. USDA: Longstalk Clover

FAMILY: Gentian (*Gentianaceae*)
GENUS: *Frasera*
SPECIES: *speciosa*
COMMON NAMES: Green Gentian, Monument Plant

FIELD NOTES: 1 stem rises from basal clump of smooth leaves. Blossoms loved by bees. Typical to find with Hellebore. Moist, open woods. 6 feet. June.

FAMILY: Geranium (*Geraniaceae*)
GENUS: *Geranium*
SPECIES: *richardsonii*
COMMON NAME: Richardson's Geranium

FIELD NOTES: Bloom 1 inch across on 3/16-inch diameter stem with blooms on top of stem. Papery blossoms visited by bees, ants, and flies. Light pink blossoms may be plants crossing with *Geranium fremontii*. Open woods. 20 inches. June.

FAMILY: Waterleaf (*Hydrophyllaceae*)
GENUS: *Phacelia*
SPECIES: *hastata*
COMMON NAME: Hastata

FIELD NOTES: Tiny leaves among blossoms with 5 petals, ½-inch stamens; blossoms funnel-shaped; velvety leaves, white-woolly. Dry, open areas. 15 inches. Mid-June.
USDA: Silverleaf Phacelia

FAMILY: Waterleaf (*Hydrophyllaceae*)
GENUS: *Phacelia*
SPECIES: *heterophylla*
COMMON NAME: Scorpion Weed

FIELD NOTES: Velvety, white-woolly, not toothed leaves. Reddish stem with white hairs. Stamens in a tight ball. Dry, sunny areas. 13 inches. Mid-June. USDA: Varileaf Phacelia

FAMILY: Lily (*Liliaceae*)
GENUS: *Calochortus*
SPECIES: *gunnisonii*
COMMON NAME: Mariposa Lily

FIELD NOTES: Grass-like stem. Not in clumps. *Mariposa* is Spanish for "butterfly." Open areas. 18 inches. June.
USDA: Gunnison's Mariposa Lily

FAMILY: Lily (*Liliaceae*)
GENUS: *Disporum*
SPECIES: *trachycarpum*
COMMON NAMES: Wartberry Fairybell, Rough-Fruited Disporum

FIELD NOTES: 2 white, narrow, 6-segment, bell-shaped, ¾-inch drooping flowers at end of forked branches. Ovate shiny leaves with no stems; reddish plant stalk. Moist, shady woods. 15–24 inches. Blossoms in mid-May; fruit is a 3-lobed, ⅜-inch yellow, then red berry, ripe in late July.

BUD

FULL BLOOM

FRUIT

FAMILY: Lily (*Liliaceae*)
GENUS: *Maianthemum*
SPECIES: *racemosum*
COMMON NAME: False Solomon's Seal

FIELD NOTES: Lustrous leaves clasp stem. Moist, shady woods. 1–3 feet. Blossoms in June–July; reddish ¼-inch berry in August–September.

FAMILY: Lily (*Liliaceae*)
GENUS: *Maianthemum*
SPECIES: *stellatum*
COMMON NAMES: Star Solomon's Seal, Star Flower

FIELD NOTES: Dainty, 6-pointed star bloom; stamen with a beige tip; lustrous, wavy, green leaves cling to stem. Aspen woods, moist areas, shady. 15 inches. Late May-June.

FAMILY: Lily *(Liliaceae)*
GENUS: *Veratrum*
SPECIES: *californicum*
COMMON NAME: White False Hellebore

FIELD NOTES: Magnificent leaves, especially stunning unfurled and emerging from ground. Many years plants wither from lack of water. Moist, open meadows and woods. Very poisonous to livestock. Stately 4-6 feet. June. USDA: False Hellebore

FAMILY: Mallow (*Malvaceae*)
GENUS: *Sidalcea*
SPECIES: *candida*
COMMON NAME: Wild Hollyhock

FIELD NOTES: Very showy l-inch blossoms in dense racemes, look like apple blossoms. Found in large patches. Moist, wet areas. 18-24 inches. June. USDA: White Checkerbloom

FAMILY: Orchid (*Orchidaceae*)
GENUS: *Corallorrhiza*
SPECIES: *maculata*
COMMON NAME: Spotted Coralroot

FIELD NOTES: Orchid with no green leaves—gets nutrients from rotting humus. Raceme of 10-30 flowers. Occurs in colonies and may disappear for years. In August, spores disperse in a cloud from dry pods. Shady woods. 12-18 inches. Late June-July. USDA: Summer Coralroot

FAMILY: Phlox (*Polemoniaceae*)
GENUS: *Ipomopsis*
SPECIES: *candida*
COMMON NAME: White Rocket Flower

FIELD NOTES: Flowers 1- to 1¼-inch long are abundant on stem. White Rocket Flower, which is found only in Colorado, is closely related to the red-blooming *Ipomopsis aggregata*. Foliage has slight skunk odor. Open woods and rocky, sunny, dry places. 24 inches. Mid-July–mid-August.

FAMILY: Phlox (*Polemoniaceae*)
GENUS: *Phlox*
SPECIES: *longifolia*
COMMON NAME: Longleaf Phlox

FIELD NOTES: Slightly woody, branching at base, delicate. Dry, sunny, rocky areas. 7–10 inches. June.

FAMILY: Buckwheat (*Polygonaceae*)
GENUS: *Eriogonum*
SPECIES: *umbellatum*
COMMON NAMES: Umbrella Buckwheat, Umbrella Plant, Subalpine Buckwheat

FIELD NOTES: Softly downy, leafless stalk arises from a basal rosette culminating in an umbel with multiple individual smaller umbels of greenish-white, 6-petal, tiny flowers, which, in bud, are raspberry red near the center of the umbel. Many *umbellatums* have several color forms and some even have flowers of a different color in the same cluster. Plants form 12–14-inch matted clumps. Rocky, sunny areas. 13 inches. Late June–July. USDA: Sulphur-Flower Buckwheat

FAMILY: Buttercup (*Ranunculaceae*)
GENUS: *Delphinium*
SPECIES: *wootoni*
COMMON NAME: Wooton's Larkspur

FIELD NOTES: Delicate; gold-yellow stamens; spur goes up, mostly basal leaves. 1 specimen. Open, sunny areas. 13 inches. Late June.

FAMILY: Buckthorn (*Rhamnaceae*)
GENUS: *Ceanothus*
SPECIES: *greggii*
COMMON NAMES: Buckbrush, Wild Lilac, Mountain Balm

FIELD NOTES: Shrub with aromatic, shiny leaves. Bush a cloud of white when in bloom. Dry, open, rocky places. 2 feet. Blossoms in mid-June; red fruit in late July.

FAMILY: Rose (*Rosaceae*)
GENUS: *Fragaria*
SPECIES: *vesca*
COMMON NAME: Wild Strawberry

FIELD NOTES: Name of genus refers to fragrance of ripe fruit in June. Fruit wasn't observed. Moist, open woods. 4 inches. Late May. USDA: Woodland Strawberry

FAMILY: Rose (*Rosaceae*)
GENUS: *Amelanchier*
SPECIES: *alnifolia*
COMMON NAME: Serviceberry

FIELD NOTES: A shrub with masses of white blossoms that when spent fall like snow; edible fruit, loved by bears. Grows in brushy clumps. Scattered throughout areas dry and moist. To 25 feet. Blossoms in May; dark blue fruit in mid-August. USDA: Saskatoon Serviceberry

FAMILY: Rose (*Rosaceae*)
GENUS: *Holodiscus*
SPECIES: *dumosus*
COMMON NAMES: Mountain Spray, Rock Spiraea

FIELD NOTES: Shrub with showy cloud of hundreds of creamy white flowers. Cliffs, rocky areas. 6 feet wide by 8 feet tall. July.

FAMILY: Rose (*Rosaceae*)
GENUS: *Prunus*
SPECIES: *virginiana*
COMMON NAME: Chokecherry

FIELD NOTES: A shrub growing in clumps of stems; sweet blossom fragrance, showy in bloom. Scattered throughout woods, meadows, and moist areas. "Choke" is in the name because when the fruit is eaten fresh it produces a puckery sensation in the mouth and throat. To 20 feet tall. Blossoms in June; dark, almost black fruit in August.

FAMILY: Rose (*Rosaceae*)
GENUS: *Rubus*
SPECIES: *idaeus*
COMMON NAME: Wild Red Raspberry

FIELD NOTES: Shrub. Rocky crevices, open woods in sunny areas. 4 feet. Blossoms in mid-June; fruit in late July.
USDA: American Red Raspberry

FAMILY: Bedstraw (*Rubiaceae*)
GENUS: *Galium*
SPECIES: *boreale*
COMMON NAME: Northern Bedstraw

FIELD NOTES: Sweet-smelling. Name derived from its use in beds. 4-sided stem, grows in large patches. Open, moist areas. 8–27 inches. Mid-June through summer.

FAMILY: Sandalwood (*Santalaceae*)
GENUS: *Comandra*
SPECIES: *umbellata*
COMMON NAME: Bastard Toadflax

FIELD NOTES: Spreads underground by roots. Dry meadows in rocky, sunny places. 10 inches. Blossoms June–July; hard, round ¼-inch stony fruit in July–August.

FAMILY: Saxifrage (*Saxifragaceae*)
GENUS: *Lithophragma*
SPECIES: *parviflorum*
COMMON NAME: Woodland Star

FIELD NOTES: *Parviflorum* means "small-flowered." Dainty herb with green "bulb" below pinkish-white, starry flowers; 10 stamens. Open slopes and meadows. 6½ inches. Late May. USDA: Smallflower Woodland-Star

FAMILY: Valerian (*Valerianaceae*)
GENUS: *Valeriana*
SPECIES: *edulis*
COMMON NAME: Western Tobacco Root

FIELD NOTES: *Edulis* means “edible”—the roots of this plant were used by American Indians for food. Lush basal leaves up to 16 inches long. Plant forms clumps to 15 inches in diameter. Moist, open woods. 4 feet. Late June. USDA: Tobacco Root

FAMILY: Valerian (*Valerianaceae*)
GENUS: *Valeriana*
SPECIES: *sitchensis*
COMMON NAME: Valerian

FIELD NOTES: Hollow stem, creamy white umbel. Moist, open woods. 1-4 feet. May-August.

FAMILY: Violet (*Violaceae*)
GENUS: *Viola*
SPECIES: *canadensis*
COMMON NAME: Canada Violet

FIELD NOTES: Purplish tinge on back of petals, purple nectar lines to yellow base of petals; heart-shaped leaves. I found a large patch in light shade on the north side of oak trees and under serviceberry branches. Moist woodlands. To 16 inches. May-June. USDA: Canadian White Violet

Yellow Flowers

FAMILY: Parsley (*Apiaceae*)
GENUS: *Lomatium*
SPECIES: *triternatum*
COMMON NAME: Lomatium

FIELD NOTES: Bright yellow, 3-4-inch umbel; grassy, thin leaf segments up to 3 inches long. Dry slopes, rocky soil, full sun. 4-19 inches. May.

FAMILY: Parsley (*Apiaceae*)
GENUS: *Osmorhiza*
SPECIES: *occidentalis*
COMMON NAME: Sweet Cicely

FIELD NOTES: Smooth, hollow stem; aromatic—smells like anise or licorice when rubbed. Moist, open woods. 2½ feet. June. USDA: Western Sweetroot

FAMILY: Aster (*Asteraceae*)
GENUS: *Agoseris*
SPECIES: *glauca*
COMMON NAME: Pale Agoseris

FIELD NOTES: Yellow petals with brownish tooth edges. Tufted appearance at center of petals. Open woods, slopes. 8 inches. June.

FAMILY: Aster (*Asteraceae*)
GENUS: *Arnica*
SPECIES: *cordifolia*
COMMON NAME: Heartleaf Arnica

FIELD NOTES: 2-3-inch blossom with 7-12 rays with 2-3 small teeth; compacted central disk. All western species have opposite leaves on flower stem. Shaded woods. 18 inches. Early June.

FAMILY: Aster (*Asteraceae*)
GENUS: *Balsamorhiza*
SPECIES: *sagittata*
COMMON NAME: Balsam Root

FIELD NOTES: Grows in handsome, showy clumps with leaves 8-20 inches long; arrowhead-shaped, soft, fuzzy leaf surface. Clumps to 3 feet in diameter on open hillsides and flats. 18 inches. May-June. USDA: Arrowleaf Balsamroot

FAMILY: Aster (*Asteraceae*)
GENUS: *Chrysothamnus*
SPECIES: *nauseosus*
COMMON NAME: Gray Rabbitbrush

FIELD NOTES: An attractive shrub. Grows in grasslands, open woodlands, and dry open areas with sagebrush. 24 inches. July.

FAMILY: Aster (*Asteraceae*)
GENUS: *Crepis*
SPECIES: *acuminata*
COMMON NAME: Hawksbeard

FIELD NOTES: Gray-green leaves to 12 inches long in basal cluster with a few smaller leaves on stalk; branched inflorescence with each flower having 11 toothed petals. Dry, open places. 30 inches. July. USDA: Tapertip Hawksbeard

FAMILY: Aster (*Asteraceae*)
GENUS: *Grindelia*
SPECIES: *squarrosa*
COMMON NAME: Curlycup Gumweed

FIELD NOTES: Blossom 1½ inches in diameter with ¾-inch sticky, gummy central disk. Tips of bracts around flowerhead strongly roll back. Dry, sunny, disturbed areas. 1–3 feet. Early August.

FAMILY: Aster (*Asteraceae*)
GENUS: *Helianthella*
SPECIES: *quinquenervis*
COMMON NAME: Sunflower

FIELD NOTES: Fuzzy, reddish stem; 4-inch blossom with 1-inch, mustard-color central disk, nodding flowers. Open woods, sunny and dry places. 4 feet. July.
USDA: Fivenerve Helianthella

FAMILY: Aster (*Asteraceae*)
GENUS: *Heliomeris*
SPECIES: *multiflora*
COMMON NAME: Golden Eye

FIELD NOTES: 8–10 petals on nodding 1-inch to 1¼-inch blossom, mustard-color center disk; prominent green bracts surround the flower bud. Dry hillsides. 8–28 inches. August–October.

FAMILY: Aster (*Asteraceae*)
GENUS: *Hymenoxys*
SPECIES: *hoopesii*
COMMON NAME: Orange Sneezeweed

FIELD NOTES: Bloom is 3 inches across; stiff, sturdy stem; fuzzy leaves and sparse petals. In bud stage, tightly closed green bracts in 1½-inch bud. Dry, sunny areas. 4 feet. Early July.

FAMILY: Aster (*Asteraceae*)
GENUS: *Krigia*
SPECIES: *biflora*
COMMON NAME: Mountain Dandelion

FIELD NOTES: A dwarf dandelion. Dry hills and open fields; found with Mule's Ears on south slopes. 12 inches. Late May. USDA: Two-Flower Dwarf Dandelion

FAMILY: Aster (*Asteraceae*)
GENUS: *Lactuca*
SPECIES: *serriola*
COMMON NAME: Wild Lettuce

FIELD NOTES: Non-native plant with a milky, sticky stem and pale spines on back of leaf rib. Dry, disturbed ground. 2–3 feet. Late July. USDA: Prickly Lettuce

FAMILY: Aster (*Asteraceae*)
GENUS: *Matricaria*
SPECIES: *discoidea*
COMMON NAME: Pineapple Weed

FIELD NOTES: A fragrant alien plant that smells like pineapple when bruised. Roadsides, waste places. 6–18 inches. Mid-June.

FAMILY: Aster (*Asteraceae*)
GENUS: *Microseris*
SPECIES: *nutans*
COMMON NAME: Wavy-Leaf Dandelion

FIELD NOTES: 13 petals with gold, tight center; reddish stems at base of plant; grass-like leaves cleft into narrow lobes. Dry meadows. 6-10 inches. May-June. USDA: Nodding Microseris

FAMILY: Aster (*Asteraceae*)
GENUS: *Packera*
SPECIES: *multilobata*
COMMON NAME: Senecio

FIELD NOTES: Basal leaves undivided; bushy basal clump with 1 stem; flower head of multiple yellow blooms with rays. Rocky, sunny areas. 6–14 inches. Mid-June. There are 100 Senecio species in the western United States, according to Spellenberg, 2001. USDA: Garden Yellowrocket

FAMILY: Aster (*Asteraceae*)
GENUS: *Senecio*
SPECIES: *crassulus*
COMMON NAME: Lambstongue

FIELD NOTES: Stout, hollow, fuzzy reddish stem. Softly toothed leaves clasp stem. Open woods, meadows. 8-28 inches. May. USDA: Thickleaf Ragwort

FAMILY: Aster (*Asteraceae*)
GENUS: *Senecio*
SPECIES: *dimorphophyllus*
COMMON NAME: Different Groundsel

FIELD NOTES: Oval basal leaves; clasping, wooly leaves on stem. Moist open areas. 15 inches. Mid-May.

FAMILY: Aster (*Asteraceae*)
GENUS: *Senecio*
SPECIES: *triangularis*
COMMON NAME: Thick-Bracted Senecio

FIELD NOTES: Sturdy, erect, stiff stem; bulging flower bracts. Grows in showy clumps. Open, sunny, dry areas. 20 inches. Late June. USDA: Arrowleaf Ragwort

FAMILY: Aster (*Asteraceae*)
GENUS: *Solidago*
SPECIES: *missouriensis*
COMMON NAME: Goldenrod

FIELD NOTES: ¼-inch multiple flowers on arching branches. Open woods, meadows. 2-3 feet. Late August.
USDA: Missouri Goldenrod

FAMILY: Aster (*Asteraceae*)
GENUS: *Taraxacum*
SPECIES: *officinale*
COMMON NAME: Dandelion

FIELD NOTES: Common dandelion. Sunny, open woods, dry or moist. 5–10 inches. Early summer.

FAMILY: Aster (*Asteraceae*)
GENUS: *Tragopogon*
SPECIES: *dubius*
COMMON NAME: Goat's Beard

FIELD NOTES: Stem below blossom is not swollen into bulge; smooth stem bearing single flower head; long, grass-like leaves; bracts less than 1 inch long. Meadows, dry areas. 12–15 inches. June–August. Magnificent seed head umbel forms in August. USDA: Yellow Salsify

FAMILY: Aster (*Asteraceae*)
GENUS: *Wyethia*
SPECIES: *amplexicaulis*
COMMON NAME: Mule's Ears

FIELD NOTES: ⅜-inch sturdy, stiff, bristly, reddish stem with handsome leaves to 15 inches long with strong leaf vein. A showy, prolific plant in clumps. Dry meadows. 2 feet. June–July.

FAMILY: Mustard (*Brassicaceae*)
GENUS: *Barbarea*
SPECIES: *vulgaris*
COMMON NAME: Winter Cress

FIELD NOTES: An alien species with tiny blossoms in leaf axils and atop stem; leaf "ears" extend to either side of smooth, soft, green stem. Moist areas. 8 inches. Late June.

FAMILY: Mustard (*Brassicaceae*)
GENUS: *Descurainia*
SPECIES: *incana*
COMMON NAME: Tansy

FIELD NOTES: Non-native, scattered everywhere. Likes disturbed dry ground. 5 feet. June.

FAMILY: Barberry (*Berberidaceae*)
GENUS: *Mahonia*
SPECIES: *repens*
COMMON NAME: Oregon Grape

FIELD NOTES: There is no obvious distinction between the *Mahonia* genus and the *Berberis* genus. Evergreen leaves, turning to red on edges; looks like holly; blossoms have sweet, beeswax fragrance. Blue fruit is edible. Rocky crevices, dry dappled shade. To 12 inches tall. Blossoms in May; fruit in July-August.

FAMILY: Forget-Me-Not (*Boraginaceae*)
GENUS: *Lithospermum*
SPECIES: *incisum*
COMMON NAME: Fringed Gromwell

FIELD NOTES: Aromatic, smells like herbicide. Dry, open areas. 2–12 inches. August. USDA: Narrowleaf Stoneseed

FAMILY: Honeysuckle (*Caprifoliaceae*)
GENUS: *Lonicera*
SPECIES: *involucrata*
COMMON NAMES: Bush Honeysuckle, Black Twinberry

FIELD NOTES: A shrub (most species of *Caprifoliaceae* are woody vines and shrubs). Damp woods, seeps. To 9 feet. Blossoms in June; berries begin to form in mid-June; berries ripe in July. USDA: Twinberry Honeysuckle

FAMILY: Pink (*Caryophyllaceae*)
GENUS: *Cerastium*
SPECIES: *glomeratum*
COMMON NAME: Chickweed

FIELD NOTES: 4–5 notched petals; flowers at stem in tight clusters. Leaves are tiny and toothed, and clasp the stem. 5 inches. May–August.

FAMILY: St. Johnswort (*Clusiaceae*)
GENUS: *Hypericum*
SPECIES: *formosum*
COMMON NAME: St. Johnswort

FIELD NOTES: Common in wet meadows, moist places. 12–32 inches. July.

FAMILY: Bean (*Fabaceae*)
GENUS: *Lathyrus*
SPECIES: *leucanthus*
COMMON NAME: Vetch

FIELD NOTES: Pea-like vines with rich, green leaves. Leaflets in pairs on stem end, with a tendril. Seeps, moist areas. 15 inches. June. USDA: Nevada Pea

FAMILY: Bean (*Fabaceae*)
GENUS: *Thermopsis*
SPECIES: *montana*
COMMON NAMES: Yellow Pea, Golden Pea

FIELD NOTES: Stout ¼-inch stalk ends in a 5-inch raceme; there are also racemes in the upper leaf axils. 3 broad, lance-like leaflets on each leaf stem. Wet, open meadows with well-drained soil. 16–40 inches. Blossoms mid-June; fruit is a 1½–3-inch slender, erect, hairy pod, in July. USDA: Mountain Goldenbanner

FAMILY: Bean (*Fabaceae*)
GENUS: *Trifolium*
SPECIES: *aureum*
COMMON NAME: Hop Clover

FIELD NOTES: An alien annual escapee, previously called *Trifolium aureum*. Trailing stems from a single root. Also known as Yellow Clover. Dry, disturbed ground. 8 inches. June–September.

FAMILY: Bean (*Fabaceae*)
GENUS: *Melilotus*
SPECIES: *officinalis*
COMMON NAME: Yellow Sweetclover

FIELD NOTES: Aggressive alien annual; fragrant, bees love it. Waste places, disturbed ground. 3-foot-long prostrate, spreading stems. June-September.

FAMILY: Fumitory (*Fumariaceae*)
GENUS: *Corydalis*
SPECIES: *aurea*
COMMON NAMES: Golden Smoke, Scrambled eggs

FIELD NOTES: Disturbed, gravelly, dry hillsides and other dry places. 5-24 inches. Late May.

FAMILY: Evening Primrose (*Onagraceae*)
GENUS: *Camissonia*
SPECIES: *tanacetifolia*
COMMON NAME: Tansyleaf Evening-Primrose

FIELD NOTES: Knob at end of style indicates it belongs in *Camissonia*, not *Oenothera*, genus. Wet meadows, places where soil is moist in spring but drying by summer. 4-6 inches. June.

FAMILY: Buckwheat (*Polygonaceae*)
GENUS: *Eriogonum*
SPECIES: *flavum*
COMMON NAME: Sulphur Flower

FIELD NOTES: Mat-forming; grows in patches; stiff stem. Dry, rocky areas. 8–16 inches. July–August. USDA: Alpine Golden Buckwheat

FAMILY: Buttercup (*Ranunculaceae*)
GENUS: *Ranunculus*
SPECIES: *abortivus*
Common Name: Kidneyleaf Buttercup

FIELD NOTES: 5 waxy, shiny petals in each ½-inch blossom, with central green cone that emerges as petals drop; drooping sepals. Open, moist areas. 12 inches. April–June. USDA: Littleleaf Buttercup

FAMILY: Buttercup (*Ranunculaceae*)
GENUS: *Ranunculus*
SPECIES: *glaberrimus*
COMMON NAME: Subalpine Buttercup

FIELD NOTES: Waxy petals; ¾-inch blossoms; petals drop soon after blossoming; short blooming time. Wet, moist. 4 inches. Very early spring.

FAMILY: Rose (*Rosaceae*)
GENUS: *Potentilla*
SPECIES: *paradoxa*
COMMON NAME: Bushy Cinquefoil

FIELD NOTES: Arrow-shaped stipules at base of leaves; bushy. Grows in clumps. Dry slopes. 18 inches. Early June.

FAMILY: Rose (*Rosaceae*)
GENUS: *Potentilla*
SPECIES: *pensylvanica*
COMMON NAME: Plains Cinquefoil

FIELD NOTES: Strawberry-like leaves prostrate on ground. Sun, partial shade, dry ground in forest and at edge of woods. 6–18 inches. June–summer.

FAMILY: Rose (*Rosaceae*)
GENUS: *Potentilla*
SPECIES: *recta*
COMMON NAME: Rough-Fruited Cinquefoil

FIELD NOTES: Silvery-backed leaves; stems fuzzy; non-native; flowers ½ – 1 inch in diameter. 15 inches. August.

FAMILY: Rose (*Rosaceae*)
GENUS: *Purshia*
SPECIES: *tridentata*
COMMON NAMES: Bitterbush, Antelope Bush

FIELD NOTES: A shrub with spreading habit; very twiggy with fragrant blossoms. Dry, rocky areas. 12–18 inches. June. USDA: Antelope Bitterbrush

FAMILY: Figwort (*Scrophulariaceae*)
GENUS: *Castilleja*
SPECIES: *puberula*
COMMON NAME: Alpine Paintbrush

FIELD NOTES: Flowers on stem top and in leaf axil; whitish hairs on lower leaves that curve and fold in on self. Sunny, dry, rocky places. 12 inches. Late June. USDA: Shortflower Indian Paintbrush

FAMILY: Figwort (*Scrophulariaceae*)
GENUS: *Castilleja*
SPECIES: *sulphurea*
COMMON NAME: Western Northern Yellow Paintbrush

FIELD NOTES: Stout stem. Moist areas, open woods. 16–20 inches. Mid-June. USDA: Sulphur Indian Paintbrush

FAMILY: Figwort (*Scrophulariaceae*)
GENUS: *Scrophularia*
SPECIES: *lanceolata*
COMMON NAMES: Bunny-in-the-Grass, Lanceleaf Figwort, Western Figwort

FIELD NOTES: Sturdy plant with clumps of basal leaves that are paired and toothed. Moist ground. 30 inches. June.

FAMILY: Figwort (*Scrophulariaceae*)
GENUS: *Verbascum*
SPECIES: *thapsus*
COMMON NAMES: Mullein, Woolly Mullein

FIELD NOTES: Non-native plant. Dry, open areas and roadsides. A noxious weed. To 6 feet. June–August. USDA: Common Mullein

FAMILY: Violet *(Violaceae)*
GENUS: *Viola*
SPECIES: *nuttallii*
COMMON NAME: Western Yellow Violet

FIELD NOTES: Moist areas in sunny, open woods. 3-5 inches. May. USDA: Nuttall's Violet

Red, Orange, and Pink Flowers

FAMILY: Dogbane (*Apocynaceae*)
GENUS: *Apocynum*
SPECIES: *androsaemifolium*
COMMON NAME: Spreading Dogbane

FIELD NOTES: Attractive, bright green leaves with ¼-inch, bell-shaped blossom that is pink-striped inside, fragrant. Dry soil, open sunny areas. 8–20 inches. Early July.

FAMILY: Aster (*Asteraceae*)
GENUS: *Agoseris*
SPECIES: *aurantiaca*
COMMON NAME: Orange Agoseris

FIELD NOTES: Fuzzy stem with reddish stripes; bud looks like Goat's Beard before blossom opens. Moist, grassy, sunny, open places. 24 inches. Late June.

FAMILY: Aster (*Asteraceae*)
GENUS: *Antennaria*
SPECIES: *rosea*
COMMON NAME: Rosy Pussytoes

FIELD NOTES: Dry, rocky, open areas. 6-8 inches. Late June.

FAMILY: Forget-Me-Not (*Boraginaceae*)
GENUS: *Cynoglossum*
SPECIES: *occidentale*
COMMON NAME: Hound's Tongue

FIELD NOTES: Fuzzy, felt-like stem with stalked lower leaves. A biennial alien. Toxic to horses and cattle. 2 feet. June.

FRUIT

FAMILY: Honeysuckle (*Caprifoliaceae*)
GENUS: *Symphoricarpos*
SPECIES: *albus*
COMMON NAME: Snowberry

FIELD NOTES: Shrub; twig-like with stiff arching branches. Paired fruit is a drupe, or seedy berry. Open woods. 3 feet. Blossoms in mid-June; fruit in August. USDA: Common Snowberry

FAMILY: Bittersweet (*Celastraceae*)
GENUS: *Paxistima*
SPECIES: *myrsinites*
COMMON NAME: Mountain Lover

FIELD NOTES: *Myrsinites* means "smells like myrrh." Handsome, evergreen leaves; $\frac{1}{8}$-inch blossoms. Fruit is a capsule; fruit not observed. Shady woods, rocky places. To 2 feet. Mid-May.

FAMILY: Bean (*Fabaceae*)
GENUS: *Lupinus*
SPECIES: *caudatus*
COMMON NAME: Pink Lupine

FIELD NOTES: Raceme is 3-4 inches; 5-7 leaf segments; smooth upper surface on leaves; ⅜-inch flowers alternate on stem. Open, grassy meadows. 14 inches. Late June. Lupinus has 600 species, according to Rickett, 1973, which hybridize, making identification difficult. This is a pink variant blooming amid a mass of blue.

FAMILY: Bean (*Fabaceae*)
GENUS: *Trifolium*
SPECIES: *wormskioldii*
COMMON NAME: Cow Clover

FIELD NOTES: *Trifolium fendleri* has larger flower heads and elliptic leaf segments. Open, grassy areas. 4–31 inches. Mid-July. USDA: Cow's Clover.

FAMILY: Gentian (*Gentianaceae*)
GENUS: *Gentianella*
SPECIES: *amarella*
COMMON NAME: Northern Gentian

FIELD NOTES: 1/32-inch blossom with tube below flower petals. Sunny, hot, dry slopes. 2–16 inches. Early June.
USDA: Autumn Dwarf Gentian

FAMILY: Geranium (*Geraniaceae*)
GENUS: *Erodium*
SPECIES: *cicutarium*
COMMON NAMES: Stork's Bill, Alfilaria

FIELD NOTES: Non-native plant; delicate. Dry areas.
4-20 inches. Mid-June.

FAMILY: Gooseberry (*Grossulariaceae*)
GENUS: *Ribes*
SPECIES: *cereum*
COMMON NAME: Wax Currant

FIELD NOTES: Shrub with pink tubular flowers with sweet, beeswax fragrance. Dry sunny, slopes. 6-8 feet. Blossoms in May-June; orange-red edible fruit in August. USDA: Alderleaf Mountain Mahogany

FAMILY: Mint (*Lamiaceae*)
GENUS: *Agastache*
SPECIES: *urticifolia*
COMMON NAME: Horse Mint

FIELD NOTES: 4-sided stem with dense terminal spike of pinkish lavender. Flower spikes also in leaf axils. Open woods and dry areas. 2–3 feet. Late June. USDA: Nettleleaf Giant Hyssop

FAMILY: Mint (*Lamiaceae*)
GENUS: *Dracocephalum*
SPECIES: *parviflorum*
COMMON NAME: Dragonhead

FIELD NOTES: Leaves have spine-tipped teeth. Seeds itself profusely on disturbed ground. Dry areas. 6–16 inches. June–September. USDA: American Dragonhead

FAMILY: Lily (*Liliaceae*)
GENUS: *Allium*
SPECIES: *acuminatum*
COMMON NAME: Wild Onion

FIELD NOTES: 21 tiny flowers with papery, white bracts and chive-like fragrance. Loose, rocky, dry soil. 4–12 inches. June. USDA: Tapertip Onion

FAMILY: Evening Primrose (*Onagraceae*)
GENUS: *Epilobium*
SPECIES: *angustifolium*
COMMON NAME: Fireweed

FIELD NOTES: Showy. Grows in clumps, burned-over areas. Bees like it. Dry, open woods. 3–4 feet. Late July.

FAMILY: Evening Primrose (*Onagraceae*)
GENUS: *Epilobium*
SPECIES: *brachycarpum*
COMMON NAME: Mouse Ears

FIELD NOTES: Delicate, thin stems. Sunny areas of dry soil. 20 inches. June.

FAMILY: Poppy (*Papaveraceae*)
GENUS: *Papaver*
SPECIES: *rhoeas*
COMMON NAME: Red Poppy

FIELD NOTES: Found once. Species from Old World. Seed pod green, egg shaped. Open sunny area. 2 feet tall, 15-inch clumps. July.

FAMILY: Phlox (*Polemoniaceae*)
GENUS: *Collomia*
SPECIES: *linearis*
COMMON NAME: Linear-Leaved Collomia

FIELD NOTES: Dry, open, sunny areas. 8 inches. Mid-June.
USDA: Tiny Trumpet

FAMILY: Phlox (*Polemoniaceae*)
GENUS: *Gilia*
SPECIES: *subnuda*
COMMON NAMES: Red Rocket Flower, Scarlet Gilia

FIELD NOTES: Biennial. Basal clump of fine leaves; 5 recurved petals form tube-like flower. Dry meadows. 18–24 inches. June.

FAMILY: Phlox (*Polemoniaceae*)
GENUS: *Ipomopsis*
SPECIES: *aggregata*
COMMON NAME: Sky Rocket

FIELD NOTES: Biennial. Bright scarlet blossom with subtle white mottling on flower lobes and 4 yellow stamens. Dry slopes, with sagebrush. 1-3 feet. Late June. USDA: Scarlet Gilia

FAMILY: Phlox (*Polemoniaceae*)
GENUS: *Phlox*
SPECIES: *viscida*
COMMON NAME: Phlox

FIELD NOTES: Grows in patches in early spring with narrow leaves and 5 petals; candy pink to pale lavender. Dry, open, sunny areas. 6 inches. May–June.

FAMILY: Purslane (*Portulacaceae*)
GENUS: *Claytonia*
SPECIES: *lanceolota*
COMMON NAME: Western Spring Beauty

FIELD NOTES: Grows from a bulb with ⅜-½-inch diameter blossom. Open, moist areas. 6-8 inches. Blooms in early May and goes to seed by mid-May. USDA: Lanceleaf Springbeauty

FAMILY: Primrose (*Primulaceae*)
GENUS: *Dodecatheon*
SPECIES: *pulchellum*
COMMON NAME: Shooting Star

FIELD NOTES: Delicate, profuse basal leaves; gorgeous, delicate blossoms. Grows in patches. Moist, wet areas. 8–14 inches. Late May–early June. USDA: Darkthroat Shootingstar

FAMILY: Rose (*Rosaceae*)
GENUS: *Rosa*
SPECIES: *nutkana*
COMMON NAME: Wild Rose

FIELD NOTES: Winged leaves at base of stem; very lovely fragrance; papery petals. Red hips, which are edible, stay on over winter. In clumps; vicious thorns. 6 feet. July. USDA: Nootka Rose

FAMILY: Rose (*Rosaceae*)
GENUS: *Sanguisorba*
SPECIES: *officinalis*
COMMON NAME: European Great Burnet

FIELD NOTES: Non-native. Grassy areas and dry meadows. 22 inches. July.

FAMILY: Rose (*Rosaceae*)
GENUS: *Rosa*
SPECIES: *woodsii*
COMMON NAMES: Smooth Rose, Sweetbriar

FIELD NOTES: Shrub with white or pink blossoms, sometimes both on same bush. Winged leaves at leaf stem; thorns hooked down. Open woods, thickets. 2–5 feet. June. USDA: Wood's Rose

FAMILY: Figwort (*Scrophulariaceae*)
GENUS: *Castilleja*
SPECIES: *linariifolia*
COMMON NAMES: Paintbrush, Wyoming Paintbrush

FIELD NOTES: Yellow form is rare. Purplish, hard stem. Open, sunny, sagebrush areas. 18 inches. Late June.
USDA: Wyoming Indian Paintbrush

FAMILY: Figwort (*Scrophulariaceae*)
GENUS: *Castilleja*
SPECIES: *miniata*
COMMON NAME: Giant Red Paintbrush

FIELD NOTES: No tri-part leaves. Dry, rocky, and grassy areas. 8-32 inches. Mid-July. USDA: Giant Red Indian Paintbrush

FAMILY: Figwort (*Scrophulariaceae*)
GENUS: *Pedicularis*
SPECIES: *procera*
COMMON NAME: Wood Betony

FIELD NOTES: Flower spike is 1 foot long; leaves to 2 feet long at base of plant, decreasing in size as they go up the stalk; reddish-purplish stout stem. Stalk grows taller as flowers mature and emerge from stalk. Moist areas. To 5 feet. July.

Blue Flowers

FAMILY: Forget-Me-Not (*Boraginaceae*)
GENUS: *Hackelia*
SPECIES: *ciliata*
COMMON NAME: Stickseed

FIELD NOTES: Incorrectly called False Forget-Me-Not. Hairy, soft leaves with tiny ⅛-inch flowers. Alien and invasive. Dry slopes. 4 feet. June–summer.

FAMILY: Forget-Me-Not (*Boraginaceae*)
GENUS: *Mertensia*
SPECIES: *oblongifolia*
COMMON NAMES: Bluebells, Foothills Bluebells

FIELD NOTES: Blossoms turn pink when fading; leaves have no stem and are wavy and smooth. Grows in clumps and often intermixed with yellow violets. Moist, open woods. 4-9 inches. Early spring.
USDA: Oblongleaf Bluebells

FAMILY: Bean (*Fabaceae*)
GENUS: *Lupinus*
SPECIES: *wyethii* or *sericeus*
COMMON NAME: Lodgepole Lupine

FIELD NOTES: Difficult to identify specific species. Dry, open woods with aspen. 2-3 feet. Mid-June. USDA: Wyeths' Lupine

FAMILY: Gentian (*Gentianaceae*)
GENUS: *Gentiana*
SPECIES: *parryi*
COMMON NAME: Parry's Gentian

FIELD NOTES: 2, 1½-inch-tall, 5-petal blossoms in terminal cluster atop a smooth stem with paired, opposite, stalkless 1½-inch leaves. Lowest leaves are shorter and ovate. The 5-pointed petals are joined with membranes cleft into 2 tiny fringes. The flowers open for only a short period each day. Lightly shaded woods. 18 inches. Mid-August–September.

FAMILY: Waterleaf (*Hydrophyllaceae*)
GENUS: *Hydrophyllum*
SPECIES: *capitatum*
COMMON NAME: Waterleaf

FIELD NOTES: Flower ball is 1½ inches in diameter; grows in profuse clumps; showy. Open woods, moist areas. 6-8 inches. May. USDA: Ballhead Waterleaf

SPRING AZURE
BUTTERFLY

FAMILY: Flax (*Linaceae*)
GENUS: *Linum*
SPECIES: *lewisii*
COMMON NAME: Flax

FIELD NOTES: Delicate soft green leaves with one main vein. Multiple green flower buds near top of flower stem bloom a few at a time for 2-3 weeks. Dry, open slopes. 2 feet. Late May-June. USDA: Lewis Flax

FAMILY: Buttercup (*Ranunculaceae*)
GENUS: *Clematis*
SPECIES: *hirsutissima*
COMMON NAMES: Leather Flower, Sugar Bowl

FIELD NOTES: Hirsute means hairy—blossom turns into fluffy seed head. Moist, open woods. 16 inches. Mid-May. USDA: Hairy Clematis

FAMILY: Buttercup (*Ranunculaceae*)
GENUS: *Delphinium*
SPECIES: *bicolor*
COMMON NAME: Larkspur

FIELD NOTES: Resembles *Delphinium nuttallianum*. Dry, open woods. 5–18 inches. Mid-May.

FAMILY: Buttercup (*Ranunculaceae*)
GENUS: *Delphinium*
SPECIES: *nelsoni*
COMMON NAME: Nelson's Larkspur

FIELD NOTES: Very pale blue blossoms; stiff stem; spur hooked down. Open hills, fields. 12 inches. June. USDA: Oregon Mountain Larkspur

FAMILY: Buttercup (*Ranunculaceae*)
GENUS: *Delphinium*
SPECIES: *nuttallianum*
COMMON NAME: Larkspur

FIELD NOTES: Spur is ½-1 inch long. Open woods. 8-12 inches. Late May. USDA: Twolobe Larkspur

FAMILY: Buttercup (*Ranunculaceae*)
GENUS: *Delphinium*
SPECIES: *occidentale*
COMMON NAME: Delphinium

FIELD NOTES: 12-inch raceme; smooth stem. Open woods, in patches. 5 feet. July.

FAMILY: Figwort (*Scrophulariaceae*)
GENUS: *Collinsia*
SPECIES: *parviflora*
COMMON NAME: Small-Flowered Collinsia

FIELD NOTES: ¼-inch blossom, 4 stamens. Moist, shady places or clearings. 6–16 inches. Mid-June.
USDA: Maiden Blue Eyed Mary

FAMILY: Figwort (*Scrophulariaceae*)
GENUS: *Penstemon*
SPECIES: *procerus*
COMMON NAME: Beardtongue

FIELD NOTES: Crowded inflorescence of drooping ½- to ¾-inch blossoms with lower lip white inside and one fuzzy yellow sterile stamen. Dry, open, rocky areas. 22 inches. Late June–early July. USDA: Pincushion Beardtongue

FAMILY: Figwort (*Scrophulariacea*)
GENUS: *Veronica*
SPECIES: *serpyllifolia*
COMMON NAME: Speedwell

FIELD NOTES: ⅛-inch blossom, 2 stamens. Moist, grassy areas. 8 inches. June. USDA: Brightblue Speedwell

Purple Flowers

FAMILY: Aster (*Asteraceae*)
GENUS: *Aster*
SPECIES: *foliaceus*
COMMON NAME: Leafy Aster

FIELD NOTES: Leaves have I vein; leaves slightly toothed. Moist, open woods and meadows. 15 inches. July-August. USDA: Parry's Aster

FAMILY: Aster (*Asteraceae*)
GENUS: *Carduus*
SPECIES: *acanthoides*
COMMON NAME: Musk Thistle

FIELD NOTES: Disturbed ground. 2 feet. Mid-July.

FAMILY: Aster (*Asteraceae*)
GENUS: *Cirsium*
SPECIES: *arvense*
COMMON NAME: Canada Thistle

FIELD NOTES: Stem has no thorns. Disturbed ground. To 6 feet. Mid-July.

FAMILY: Aster (*Asteraceae*)
GENUS: *Erigeron*
SPECIES: *glabellus*
COMMON NAME: Smooth Daisy

FIELD NOTES: 1¼-inch-diameter blossom, ½-inch center disk; fringy, profuse petals; stiff stem with leaves longer at bottom of stem. Moist areas. 15–18 inches. June–August. USDA: Streamside Fleabane

FAMILY: Aster (*Asteraceae*)
GENUS: *Erigeron*
SPECIES: *speciosus*
COMMON NAMES: Showy Fleabane, Blue Aspen Daisy

FIELD NOTES: Showy in large patches and swaths of plants. Dry areas. 18 inches. Late June–August. USDA: Aspen Fleabane

FAMILY: Aster (*Asteraceae*)
GENUS: *Erigeron*
SPECIES: *subtrinervis*
COMMON NAME: Threenerve Fleabane

FIELD NOTES: Leaves have 3 veins; fringy look because of profuse flower rays; blue to pink 1½-inch flower with ⅜-inch center disk; bracts lined up side by side. Woodland openings. 12–15 inches. Early August.

FAMILY: Aster (*Asteraceae*)
GENUS: *Onopordum*
SPECIES: *acanthium*
COMMON NAME: Scotch Thistle

FIELD NOTES: Disturbed ground. 3 feet. Early July.
USDA: Scotch Cottonthistle

FAMILY: Aster (*Asteraceae*)
GENUS: *Symphyotrichum*
SPECIES: *campestre*
COMMON NAMES: Field Aster, Prairie Aster

FIELD NOTES: 1 main leaf vein, leaves not deeply clasping the stem; bloom 1 inch in diameter with 30 rays, ⅜-inch disk; base of petals white. Very prolific and widely spread. Dry, open areas. 2 feet. June–September.

SEED UMBEL

FAMILY: Aster (*Asteraceae*)
GENUS: *Tragopogon*
SPECIES: *porrifolius*
COMMON NAMES: Salsify, Oyster Plant

FIELD NOTES: Stem is swollen and hollow just below flower head. Edible root that can be cultivated. Because blossom closes at mid-day, it is known in England as Jack-Go-to-Bed. 24 inches. July. Seed umbel forms in August.

FAMILY: Bean (*Fabaceae*)
GENUS: *Lupinus*
SPECIES: *sericeus*
COMMON NAME: Lupine

FIELD NOTES: A difficult to identify group of species with showy, 6-inch flower racemes. Open woods, meadows. 18-34 inches. May-June. USDA: Silky Lupine

FAMILY: Bean (*Fabaceae*)
GENUS: *Vicia*
SPECIES: *americana*
COMMON NAMES: American Vetch, Blue or Purple Vetch

FIELD NOTES: Open woods and meadows. 12 inches. June–August.

FAMILY: Geranium (*Geraniaceae*)
GENUS: *Geranium*
SPECIES: *viscosissimum*
COMMON NAMES: Sticky Geranium, Wild Geranium, Crane's Bill

FIELD NOTES: Papery pale lavender blossoms. Dispersed in open woods. Insects love them. 1-3 feet. Mid-June. USDA: Sticky Purple Geranium

FAMILY: Waterleaf (*Hydrophyllaceae*)
GENUS: *Phacelia*
SPECIES: *sericea*
COMMON NAMES: Purple Fringe, Silky Phacelia, Alpine Phacelia

FIELD NOTES: 6-inch dense terminal spike with bristly appearance; rigid, hollow, ¼-inch stem. Dry, rocky soil. 20 inches. Late June. USDA: Silky Phacelia

FAMILY: Evening Primrose (*Onagraceae*)
GENUS: *Epilobium*
SPECIES: *coloratum*
COMMON NAME: Purple-Leaved Willow-Herb

FIELD NOTES: Ridged stem often purplish; erect maroon pods, 2½ inches long. Wet, marshy places. 12–15 inches. Late June.

FAMILY: Figwort (*Scrophulariaceae*)
GENUS: *Penstemon*
SPECIES: *strictus*
COMMON NAME: One-Sided Penstemon

FIELD NOTES: Among sagebrush and dry, gravelly slopes; bees crawl inside blossoms. To 32 inches. Mid-June-July.
USDA: Rocky Mountain Penstemon

FAMILY: Violet (*Violaceae*)
GENUS: *Viola*
SPECIES: *adunca*
COMMON NAME: Early Blue Violet

FIELD NOTES: Leaves fold toward each other at leaf base above stem; I leaf per stem with blossom on separate stem. Found in clumps. Open woods. 2-5 inches. Mid-May-June. USDA: Hookedspur Violet

Green and Brown Flowers

FAMILY: Aster (*Asteraceae*)
GENUS: *Rudbeckia*
SPECIES: *occidentalis*
COMMON NAMES: Western Coneflower, Naked Coneflower

FIELD NOTES: Clumps 30 inches across; profuse basal leaves. Moist, open woods. 2–5 feet. June–August.

FAMILY: Buckwheat (*Polygonaceae*)
GENUS: *Rumex*
SPECIES: *crispus*
COMMON NAME: Curly Dock

FIELD NOTES: Non-native.Wavy leaf edges. Greenish-pink then browns when flowers mature. Moist, wet areas. 12–40 inches. Late July.

FAMILY: Buttercup (*Ranunculaceae*)
GENUS: *Thalictrum*
SPECIES: *fendleri*
COMMON NAMES: Early Meadow-Rue, Fendler's Meadow-Rue

FIELD NOTES: Stiff, hard stem with fern-like foliage. Open woods. 24 inches. June–July.

FAMILY: Cattail (*Typhaceae*)
GENUS: *Typha*
SPECIES: *latifolia*
COMMON NAME: Cattail

FIELD NOTES: Staminate spike immediately above the pistillate, a velvety brown cylinder. Ponds, ditches. To 8 feet. Late July. USDA: Broadleaf Cattail

AFTERWORD

I was born in a small town in central Wisconsin. I grew up and lived most of my life there. I stayed in Wisconsin for many years raising my children. During that time I earned a master of arts degree at the University of Wisconsin. But I had always loved Colorado, so in February of 1990, I acquired the land upon which this book is based. My family and I built a 16-foot-by-20-foot cabin on that land in August of that year. I moved to Colorado in November of 1993, and I spent an adventurous winter in the cabin. Propane lights, an outhouse, and a spring for water provided primitive—but sufficient—amenities. However, I needed telephone service, mail delivery, and electricity to maintain my business as an artist. To fulfill these needs, I moved to Grand Junction in May of 1994, and that location serves as my home base. Since then, I live at the cabin from spring through fall, and spend the winters in Grand Junction.

REFERENCES

Britton, Nathaniel Lord, and Hon. Addison Brown. *An Illustrated Flora of the Northern United States and Canada.* 2nd Edition, in Three Volumes. New York: Dover Publications, 1970.

Craighead, John J., and Frank C. Craighead, Jr., Ray J. Davis. *Field Guide to Rocky Mountain Wildflowers.* Cambridge: The Riverside Press, 1963

Ells, James. *Rocky Mountain Flora.* Golden, CO: The Colorado Mountain Club Press, 2006.

Guennel, G.K. *Guide to Colorado Wildflowers, Mountains.* Volume 2. Englewood, CO: Westcliffe Publishers, 1995.

———. *Guide to Colorado Wildflowers, Plains & Foothills.* Volume 1. Englewood, CO: Westcliffe Publishers, 1995.

Integrated Taxonomic Information System website: www.itis.gov.

Pavia, Jerry. *Rocky Mountain Wildflowers.* Golden, CO: Fulcrum Publishing, 2003.

Peterson, Roger Tory, and Margaret McKenny. *A Field Guide to Wildflowers of Northeastern and Northcentral North America.* Illustrations by Roger Tory Peterson. Boston: Houghton Mifflin Co, 1968.

Pesman, M. Walter. *Meet the Natives, A Beginner's Field Guide to Rocky Mountain Wildflowers, Trees and Shrubs.* 10th Edition. Boulder: Roberts Rinehart Publishers, 1992.

Rickett, Harold William. *Wild Flowers of the U.S.* Volume 6, Parts One, Two, Three. *The Central Mountains and Plains.* General Editor: William C. Steere. Publication of the New York Botanical Garden. New York: McGraw-Hill, 1973.

Roberts, Rhoda, and Dr. Ruth Aston Nelson. *Colorado Wildflowers.* Museum Pictorial No. 8. Publications Department of Denver Museum of Natural History. Denver: Bradford-Robinson Printing, 1957.

Robertson, Leigh. *Southern Rocky Mountain Wildflowers, a Field Guide to Common Wildflowers, Shrubs & Trees.*

Text by Leigh Robertson. Photos by Duane B. Squires and others. Guildord, CT: The Globe Pequot Press, 1999.

United States Department of Agriculture website: www.plants.usda.gov.

Spellenberg, Richard. *Field Guide to North American Wildflowers, Western Region.* National Audubon Society, Revised Edition. Professor Emeritus of Biology, New Mexico State University. New York: Alfred A. Knopf, 2001.

Taylor, Ronald J. *Rocky Mountain Wildflowers.* Beaverton, OR: The Touchstone Press, 1978.

Taylor, Ronald J. *Sagebrush Country, A Wildflower Sanctuary.* Missoula, MT: Mountain Press Publishing, 1992.

Troublesome Weeds of The Rocky Mountain West. Colorado Weed Management Association, 2002.

Young, Robert G., and Joann W. Young 1977. *Colorado West, Land of Geology & Wildflowers.* Grand Junction, CO: Wheelwright Press, 1977.

INDEX OF COMMON NAMES

INDEX OF LATIN NAMES